hearts of the earth

a collection of poems // morgan raeshel short

Printed in the United States of America
First Printing, 2021
ISBN 978-1-949321-26-5

All writings within this book belong to the author.
Cover Art & Design by: Jamie Boucher

A.B.Baird Publishing
66548 Highway 203
La Grande OR, 97850
USA
www.abbairdpublishing.com

to all those with infinite love in their hearts.

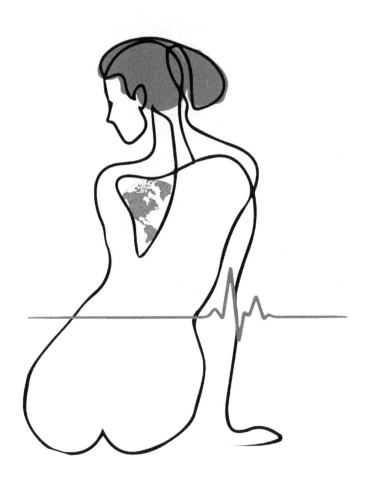

how hearts of the earth emerged

i read once about how love poetry was overdone. maybe. but if love poetry is overdone, why do we keep reading it? if love songs are written too often, why do we sing them at the top of our lungs? *whitney. adele. celine.* why do names become rallying cries? *jolene. roxanne. virginia.* if we're tired of watching the same damn love story on the hallmark channel, then why does hallmark keep making the same damn movie? why do you ache when noah and allie die in each other's arms? why do you smile when johnny says *nobody puts baby in the corner*? when lloyd holds a boombox over his head, while serenading diane?

the truth is, love stories may be overdone. love poetry may be overdone. but love never is. we create art about love because there are countless love stories. thousands of hearts of the earth.

hearts that are *beating.* hearts that are *wandering.* hearts that are *falling. loving. breaking. healing. manifesting.*

so these are a handful of odes to my heart, in each of its phases. and to all of the hearts of the earth, in each of their phases. maybe you'll see some of your own story in it. maybe in the end, you'll conclude this is just another poetry book about love and heartache. maybe you'll conclude it was just a book about a girl looking for love in all the wrong places. that love was inside her all along, all she had to do was reach in to get it. whatever your conclusion, *i hope you feel something.*

so then, if love is what you want from the universe,
love is what your hand shall give to it

beating

breathe in
realize you are incredibly alive breathe out
remember that is a miracle itself

// look how every breath saves you

can we just pause
touch the earth wildly
let the roots reach our souls
love each other deeply
til our hearts become whole
share our truths always
our stories to be told
can we just live
can we just be

// wandering earth's roots

a starving ego
craving far more than mediocrity
an untamed soul
seeking anything
but ordinary

// not interested in average

the sun has this power
its rays have this way
of lifting the weight of the world
off your shoulders
just let it shine down on you
let it shower you with joy

// rain isn't the only one who showers

i carved my initials in its core, it grounded me
i liked being in both places at once
but i knew to reach the top
i'd have to promise to never look down
to rise i had to lift my feet off the ground

// willow

you ask me to pour out my soul
like a cup would be able to hold it

where can i look to find my identity

i could look to my reflection
but all i'd see is a body that holds it

maybe i could find it in my shadow
following me and collecting its shape
from my past's darkest moments

maybe i'd find it in the labels
my community takes comfort in assigning me

you ask me to tell you who i am
like my identity is tangible, like it's static
perhaps i'm just the summation of my experiences

// identity quest

she got lost searching for meaning
until she tucked her yearning for meaning
in her back pocket
and let her existence lead the way

// they call them coincidences

your heart is beating
    why
you're among other humans on this earth
       why
you've been given a century of human life
              what the hell are you going to do with it

// find your why

what if we're not humans experiencing love, afterall
what if we're love experiencing what it's like to be human

// love beings

is it nature or nurture
how we learn about love
is it stitched into our spirits
mapped into our DNA
or is love only realized
through human connection

// love's conception

if you stripped it all away
rid yourself of everything
friends, lovers, your nine to five
filters, consumerism, appearances, wine
if you stood there on the earth
tip toeing in the mud
no other beating hearts around
tell me this
would you be lonely
or would you just be alone
tell me are you comfortable
in the presence of your own soul
are you ready to hear
every little thing it desires
or are you terrified

// bare soul

one - embrace change
    two - if it no longer serves you, let it go
        three - when it feels like you've lost everything,
        remember your roots
            four - it's a beautiful thing, baring your soul

// life lessons from autumn trees

which me should set sail
when i am lost at sea
the sweet child
hoping for serendipity
or the mature woman
willing to face reality

// i am many ships

amidst the sun
a dark rain cloud
the forest quiet
her heart loud

// sunny with a chance of heartache

softly surrendering her spirit
willingly walking the way
not an eye on the end game
wanderers need not worry
wanderers need not plan
hear how the birds sing
breathe easy, let it be

// surrender

wandering

if what they say is true
and i have to wait
til my own soul is whole
before i meet you
then i guess i better start
wandering

// soul searcher

if we were all just wandering souls
released from our bodies
how different love would be
love sans physical attraction
can you imagine
our souls just flying
like a flock of birds
alas, it is only the nature
of earth's creatures
to notice those with
the most beautiful feathers

// soul searcher part II

it's as if i am looking
for a place to put my heart
like i will not rest
til i find a soul to keep it
to tame it
to be powerless in love
how funny a thing
yet somehow still desirable

// powerless heart

we are all just floating hearts
looking for another heart to call home
some tied together by ribbons of love
others traveling through space
hoping to find another before they pop

// balloon hearts

humans are funny that way
how we embrace love as the culmination
the pinnacle of human existence
like we are not living, if we are not loving

// i am breathing, so i am living

love was on the horizon
but she refused to set sail
instead she walked the shore
searching for love
as if it were a sand dollar
forgetting the ocean's
many treasures

// x marks the spot

the sun the moon and the stars
always the main attraction
forgotten is the soil
nourishing the plants
fueling the animals that walk this land
the woman who gives her love to the man
why have they all gone unnoticed
alas, another one is his focus
she pours out her heart
but she and the sun are worlds apart

// she is not the sun

if people can fall in love
do you think I could just
trip someone
right into love with me
or is that too forceful
likely the latter
but in the end
maybe it doesn't matter
as long as they fall gracefully

// armed with cupid's arrow

there's so much love inside this chest
looking for a place to finally rest
all locked away and i've thrown out the key
yes i can hear it cry and feel its ache
but when my heart leaves its safe haven
it usually breaks

// restless heart

she has this enchantment about her
her smile alone says
loving me will make you feel alive

// where can I find the spell for her magic

god, are you out there
please send new muse
and if it's not a bother
one with good intentions
affirming words
and positive vibrations

// amen

doubting the love of another
is her mind's greatest burden
she wanders through fields
plucking the petals
of love me, love me not's
until the fields are bare
and love has nowhere left to blossom

// flower child

awaiting her story
made her jaded
she grew used to
solo ventures
and relished in the
silence of solitude
cynically believing
she would never
be cast as a juliet

// where's romeo

love songs i can handle
but i'm no friend of fairy tales
i guess it's the way they paint the princess
can someone write her a better plot
something more deserving
than sleeping until she's kissed

// aurora

seven point six seven four billion
people in this world
and you're supposed to find the *one*
engineered perfectly for you
what if my soulmate is in the last frontier

// hey siri, show me flights to alaska

my morning coffee
left me wanting more today
or maybe it was the rain
or the music
the mug
the precipitation
bon iver on repeat
something about it all
made me crave a shoulder
to rest my head on
a hand
to give my fingers to

// french vanilla

craving the sweet taste
of his name on my lips
a name i've yet to say
a thirst left unquenched

// just one sip

with changing seasons
our morals fell

// so call us autumn sinners

she sipped her citrus moscato
then her thumb traced the rim of the glass
like wine, his words were sweet on the surface
but she knew what was coming next
he'd pump her full of cheap liquor and meaningless words
anything to move the party to the bedroom
he was the type of man
who hid his intentions behind forehead kisses
the type to cry *good guys finish last*
she could see right through him
so before departing, she opted for one more glass
she unscrewed the cork and stained her lips red
something darker, a taste to match his disguise
never hearing from him again would be no surprise

// empty calories, small talk

seducing silence
drenched in temptation
alluring eyes
earned my fixation

// lust

somewhere between
the what if's and the how to's
i found you
and it wasn't long before
i succumbed to temptation
in moments of desperation
offering what was only mine
hands tracing every inch of my spineless spine
morals forsaken
my body, your taking
but make no mistake
you were but a guest in my temple

// worship

she longed for the enchanting moon
still the sun was the one to kiss her

// and it burned

falling

i'd call it a whimsical paradox
how the consequence of falling in love
is either another inevitable departure
or the one who stays forever

// which one will this be

let's just blame love on gravity
an invisible force
pulling objects toward each other
making us fall

// earth's astronauts

the wanderers told us stories
about the ones who jumped
how despite the dark abyss
they leaped and found bountiful bliss

// base jumpers

what if this fall breaks every bone in my body
what if the parachute doesn't open like you promised
will you take my hand and jump with me

// into our love story

i'm terrified that following your voice
out of this maze
will mean leaving my own behind
please don't let me leave my livelihood
in these strands of grass

// i don't want to lose myself

you tell me not to worry, that you're nothing like the other lovers. but i don't think you understand. i'm not usually a fan of cliches, but it was me, not him.

i know how it all looks. i look defeated, discouraged, and unhappy. you think he must have been horrible to me. the truth is, i was horrible to myself. i fell so hard into him, embracing him as my entire universe. and somewhere along that journey of loving too hard and giving too much, i no longer recognized myself.

and that's why i'm scared to fall again. because i absolutely adore the life i've created for myself. i don't want to let it slip through my fingers.

// unrecognizable

my bones can't swim at the surface
they can only dive into the depths of oceans
i can't just float with you on cloud nine
i'd rather find a rainbow and paint the entire sky
please forgive my unforgiving intensity

// i don't just fall, i plummet

i can't play the game. i don't know what halfway means. i don't know how to be casual or just go with it.

any sign of love rushes through my veins like venom and i awaken. when my blood recognizes that familiar high, i'm an addict all over again.

i don't know how to be anything but too much, too fiery, too passionate. and i will not play pretend. i will not dismiss my feelings just to avoid a bruised ego. i'll tell you. i'll show you. i'll go all in and bet on us. i'll make it clear as day. and then you'll run away.

at least that's what most people do when they meet my intensity.

// they leave

we collect
the daggers
bullets
and arrows
of the past
as armor
shielding us
from giving
love a chance

// weaponry

something about you, though
makes me want to
retire this old suit of armor
face every battle
hand in hand

// soldiers unshielded

i go to share my truth
but my voice trembles with unease
how do i find the words
to finally make you believe
perhaps a letter would suit this better
funny how letters can make voices heard
sometimes i get lucky with written words

// you have me tongue tied

would i bet on us
should i go all in
i'd need a royal flush
to silence any doubts
who knows if you're bluffing

// will we fold or will we fall

you stole my thoughts the moment i met you
i couldn't register a doubt, because my mind wasn't even mine
you said let go of fear, i did without hesitancy
you commanded me to fall, i fell relentlessly
you encouraged my intensity
you had me in a trance, enchanted

// hypnotist

where the heaven did you come from
and can you please stay

// angelic

you're too good to be true

no one had ever said those words to me before
your words knocked me on my feet
i'm too good to be true
you mean you had been searching for exactly me
you had drawn me up in your dreams
i couldn't believe it
those words made me feel more loved than any *i love you* ever had

// so i am somebody's somebody

you've piqued my interest
that's an understatement

i'm consumed by you
that's more like it

i can't deny it
there's an entire world to be perceived
and all i can see is you

// falling into you

i know it sounds silly but
yesterday you said you wanted tacos
instead, you ate a burger
what if i'm like the tacos
people change their minds all the time
and it's terrifying

// foodie

he's a bulldozer entering your world
happily and recklessly demolishing
every wall you've ever-so-carefully crafted
as your walls fall to the ground
he'll build you up in their place and if anyone tries
to knock you down when you're vulnerable and without walls
he'll be there as the strongest pillar of protection
and the softest place to fall

// construction site

i want to know you
between every line
behind every door
among other beings
and all alone
i want to hear
your wildest dreams
and your faintest memories
tell me your story
write it in permanent marker
stay forever

// to learn and to love

energy pouring through your veins
blood rushing to your head
his tongue tied, a constrictor knot
his cheeks flushed, bright red
keep the flame burning

// fiery passion

free falling from level ninety four
mind on fire, i want more
thoughts like ashes, scattered
veins pierced with fresh matter
new wave, abundant energy
it's all clear now, meant to be

// the fall

loving

they say we're crazy
i say we're just crazy enough
to see how this little world of ours
orbits in this galaxy of hidden stars

// universal love

i found my home in your eyes
they told me i was seen here
they told me i was safe here
they said a million enchanting words
and i got lost in their infinite meanings

// love lived in your eyes

i know this might sound crazy but -

but what?

i'd never seen you wear a smile that way before
you looked up at the open road
back at me, then back at the road again
your smile never wavered

ah, nothing

it wasn't nothing
it was everything
that was the first time you told me you loved me
and i said it back when i laughed
and squeezed your hand tight

// driven to love

have you ever met someone and thought,

i have loved you before

what if i told you *love at first sight*
is just a concept we made up
because we're too uncomfortable with the idea
that maybe our souls loved each other in a different universe
and we were always destined to find each other's hearts again

// in this dimension

i remember that saturday. we played and paused music all day. you lit up about your favorite songs and you were so curious to know mine. we deconstructed the lyrics. reminisced on shows we had seen. festivals we had attended. i loved learning about how music moved you. i could have stayed in those moments with you forever.

we talked about planning new music adventures together. we would have booked a flight to colorado for a show at red rocks right then and there, had it not conflicted with my calendar.

i'm not sure why that day sticks out in my brain. all we did was listen to music. but it brought us together. you might even say it taught us how to love each other.

// music is love

i can't sleep
because i can't stand
spending eight hours without you
people go insane from sleep deprivation
but i'm already madly in love with you

// when reality is better than your dreams

love has a million different meanings
and yet somehow we all crave a single feeling
to be wanted, to be seen
i've always struggled with describing what love means
but you sure do make me feel it

// it's a feeling

a filtered view
won't let me indulge
in the wonders of you
pour me a stiff glass of your soul
feed me your fears
whisper your secrets in my ears
inject your faintest memories in my veins
show me all the things my eyes can't see
give me the strongest dose of you

// stoned on you

even their umbrellas
couldn't protect them from
the torrential downpour of love
so they ditched their shields
and felt the love
hit their heads
and their faces
and their hearts
they let it pour
arms wide open

// drenched in love

and as my father serenades my mother
taking her into his arms for a slow dance
i see them fall young
twenty five years younger
a dapper young fella
leaning against a building
waiting for his charming woman
she smiles at him then
and i think right in that moment he knew
he'd be dancing with her forever

// jodi

somewhere across the electric sky
rhythmic melodies
beating from cloud nine
harmonic hums
seeping through, synchronized

// where lovers roam

call it what you want
lyrical beauty sent straight from above
a heavenly justice
a beacon of hope
call it a coincidence if you choose to
a miracle if that suits you
as for me, i'm going to do as the skies do

// blue

i never intended on saying this again
but here i am, and here we are
giving the same three words
an entirely different meaning
a brand new tune to dance to

// another lover

love is not a security blanket
or a choice you make
or a person you spend your time with
love is not a settlement
or a partner in crime
or indulging in each other under the sheets
love is so much more

call it far fetched or maybe a little naive
but when i hear

i love you

i hear

i see your soul
i understand every fiber of your being
i know what fuels your fire
i see the light in your spirit, and i will never do anything to put it out
keep burning baby, i see you

maybe asking for a love like that makes me complicated, or layered
maybe it even makes me hard to love
but i won't apologize for wearing my heart on my sleeve
i spent years burying my spirit, letting dirty shoes walk all over it
if you want to love me, please don't leave me buried

// love me for how i love this life

it's tricky for me to write about love. the relationship kind, i mean.

do i believe in love as a concept? absolutely. i've seen the others. how their souls seem to exist exactly for each other. i've watched how they build one another up and make each other better. i've seen how their smiles sing for their love.

and yes, i know what it means to love your mom, your sister, and your best friend. but let's leave that kind of love for another time.

love love, is hard for me to grasp and difficult for me to write about. i suppose that's because every time i write about love, i can't help but contextualize it around heartache. for me they go hand in hand. always have.

listen, i'd love to be the poet who writes about the genuine, world-shaking, mind-blowing kind of love. but something about writing about love in that way makes me feel like a bit of an imposter - since i haven't found it yet.

maybe someday i'll find that kind of love. the one that ends my wandering. the kind my mom and dad have. maybe then i'll author one hundred books about earth shattering love and fill libraries with them.

// until then

breaking

each of you left me with a broken heart and another lesson.

you introduced me to heartache...

be careful with what you do with my heart,
if you break it, you'll turn into poetry.

// a cautionary tale

i wouldn't wish it on anyone, a broken heart
and yet, some damaged part of mine
can't handle the thought of
the hearts of the heartbreakers
going untouched

// moralistic heart

numbness
set across her skin
a protective layer
made of broken promises
and no one could touch her
even if she let them

// anesthesia

i don't know why you stood there
barefoot among wood chips
one of them was bound
to give you a splinter

// vulnerable

the vinegar aroma exposed you first
then the glass gave its clue when it shattered
your promises taste like bad wine

// bitter

a symbol of love or a handful of lies
our love like those roses
was destined to die

// you always chose roses

speaking of roses,
i remember my birthday one year
you gave me a single fake rose
you said something about not choosing a real rose
because even though a real rose was as real as your love for me,
it would eventually dry and wither
so you chose a fake rose because it would never fade
just like i would never fade from your heart or mind
so the fake rose represented eternal love, right?

// oh honey, you chose wrong

the difference between
you and the winter
one is chilly
the other is relentlessly cold

// your cold heart

how do i take
all these things i have learned
and open my arms for love again
when the first lesson you taught me
was i was forever loved
and the last lesson you taught me
was that the first was a lie

// bad teacher

i remember the nights he serenaded me
his brown eyed girl loved him tirelessly
and then he ended it, seeking solitude
a desire that apparently escaped him
when he met you only months later

so yes, i had a few physical reactions to hearing the news
when i learned he had chosen you
headache, sore throat, face flushed beat red
drenched in remorse and self-pity

he seems different now though, with you i mean
maybe you're it, i certainly wasn't
but maybe i can help you love him the way he needs you to love
him, while he's yours

so, take it from me
when his song comes on the radio, sing your heart out with him
when he gets overwhelmed in a big crowd, give him space
pull him out of his comfort zone, but not all at once
explore new places, take him on adventures
fuel spontaneity into his rigid plans
his generosity is authentic
he'll flood you with romantics, embrace them
in the moments when you're feeling down,
he'll look into your eyes and tell you to keep your chin up
cause it's easier to kiss you that way
when he tells you you're beautiful, he means it
when he builds you up, it's pure

but when he makes you a promise, challenge him
take *i love you* with a grain of salt
be careful with his promises
because, from my experience,
some promises, he just can't keep

// to the new girl that has his heart

you taught me about unrequited love…

how foolish of me to believe
you were indebted to me
only because i so effortlessly
gave you my heart to handle
i am sorry for believing
you owed me yours in return
please forgive my wandering love
for it is only searching
for arms to call home

// apology

the funny thing about love is that
it's not always enough
sometimes it is wasteful
sometimes unfulfilled
sometimes heart wrenching
tear-filled and unkind
sometimes it shows up
at the exact wrong time
just to take your heart and
leave it fluttering there
right in the air
not even love's to break

// wasted love

you were the composer, i was a note
you wrote me into your song
next to all your other notes
and we were all to work together
in perfect harmony, for you
but dissonance was inevitable
you were once a composer
now you're a clown
go ahead clown,
juggle all your notes

// crescendo

i am a loose leaf piece of paper
used once for your convenience
a disposal for your thoughts
crinkled up and tossed in the wastebasket

// post it note

how vibrant my mind would be
if it weren't oversaturated
with thoughts of you

// photographic heart

and with impending change
nothing seems constant
but the certainty
that I will continue
dreaming of you

// change and certainty

how is it that my heart
who ignores the inevitable
and chases the improbable
is the one convincing my head
it is delusional

// heart and mind tricks

it was on the tip of my tongue for so long, tickling the same way whiskey does when you're on your second and ordering your third.

some time after my third i finally realized that i don't like how it feels when i let you pour the shots.

i couldn't put my finger on it, cause you kept lifting yours and pointing in the direction you wanted me to go. i would have followed you anywhere if you would have let me.

i think i've finally found my own path, not forged by you. tomorrow, i'm blazing the trails and heading straight north.

// just north of whiskey

my heart, you silly thing do not flutter for those incapable of receiving. today, my heart, i challenge you to love in ways unfamiliar to you, in ways that bring only joy.

no more sorrow, sweet heart of mine. you are released from the chains of unreturned love. oh how those chains weighed you down for so long.

no worry, my heart. unreturned love is no bother to a heart pumping on its own. be free, my heart. run wild, fly high. be selfish, my heart, find your adventure.

// unchained heart

you made wonder what could have been...

we fell apart softly, quietly. the way rain sounds when it hits the creek's surface. gracefully. creating a sort of ambience.

but falling for you was not quiet. no. with you i learned a charming melody. your rhythm made me wild. i fell into it hard.

i forget the way it sounded though. i suppose i only knew it awhile. it comes back to me sometimes. in moments like these. when my head is clear and earth's beauty hits me right between the eyes. that's when the longing for the music hits me hardest.

maybe i think of you in these moments because yours is the most recent tune i knew. perhaps, i'll find a new one soon. beat every drum and pluck every string until the clustered sounds make some kind of melody i can keep.

// our souls made music

a red rose. saturdays. my favorite tune. i write out all the metaphors i can think of to describe how what we had died too soon. how sometimes the most delicious fruits have the closest expiration dates.

you see, i search for meaning in everything. searching for some definition. some reason why.

and when the answer is blank, when the results are inconclusive, i panic. why did you get to open me up? make me feel alive? how come those before you were greeted with brick walls and you an open door? why did i let you in? and why did you leave so soon?

i'm in the business of writing stories, but i can't finish this one on my own. i can't even decipher the language we wrote our story in. so i'm filing it away on a shelf where, for now, it will simply collect dust. and soon, once again, it will be time to write fresh pages.

// dust collector

you dug the grave
when you left
and I guess I surrendered
when I threw them in

// here lies our buried dreams

the droplet is all that remains
quiet repetition, soft falls
a sign of life, after all
but only a dripping droplet
from the faucet
between these brick walls

// love in the kitchen sink

499 puzzle pieces
11:59 p.m.
half an ounce of vodka
this numbness
you and me
something about it all
feels so
unended

// that's not what they mean by everlasting love, right?

vodka spilled from the shattered glass
upon her bedside table
falling onto the letter
she wrote the night before
a letter she couldn't salvage
a truth she'd never send
there was no courage anyway
red eyes, unrest, unwell, she thinks...
i am hungover because i am hung up on you

// absolut bottom

unlike the others, i never lost myself in you
although, you were the one i lost soonest
i let you slip almost before you were mine to begin with
i imagine somewhere, somehow our flame is still burning

// twin flame

i see you happy with her now. she's happy too, i can tell. how am i?

well, it was a deep ache at first. a longing for what could have been. confusion from the whiplash. one moment you were talking about moving in, the next you were moving on. and even though i'm lonely most days, i really only feel two emotions when i think of you. nostalgia and happiness.

except it's not nostalgia for the past. it's nostalgia for what's coming and all the hope i have for the future. thinking of you makes me happy because i know exactly what it's supposed to feel like. love i mean. during our short-lived romance, i never told you i loved you. but i'm pretty certain i did. i told all the others i loved them, but after feeling what i felt when i was with you, i'm not sure i meant it.

with the others, the words bubbled up without warning. *i love you*, i said. but what i meant was i love the attention. i love that someone wants me. i love feeling safe and chosen.

if i would have said those words to you, they would have meant, i love how you love life. i love how you go after what you want, even if it's unconventional. i love how you can make a total stranger your instant friend. that feels a lot closer to the meaning of the words i love you. when i said it to all the others, i think i meant *i love that you love me*.

// does that make me a liar

you took my heart and left empty promises in return...

the more i learn
the less i know
nothing's adding up
subtract your words
the remainder's your actions
maybe the problem
is a faulty equation
maybe the problem is
me + you

// mathematically speaking

we rode the tide of sweet oblivion
all the way through to the very end
nothingness, our comforting friend
like children we played pretend
we both knew it was only temporary
and time was our looming enemy

// it had to end

the differences don't show up in the loneliness
they show up in the comfort we find
when the loneliness subsides

in loneliness we share desire and pain
angst and even heartache
past memories haunting us
wonders of love ever finding us again

in comfort we diverge
you in your element, singing haunted melodies
me in my head
thinking up idealist possibilities

i suppose in a way you are like salt
which i guess would make me honey

// salt and honey

we tiptoed down a path of rose petals, leading to a locked door
you had the key, but left it in your pocket
imagine what we would have uncovered beyond that locked door
instead, i'm standing here barefoot on thorns

// bleeding

there's something about wine-stained lips
that make me want to say
the most loving, hateful things

// truth serum

i said it was over
but you meant it
silence said it all
wish i had dreamt it
i lit the fire
you watched it burn
sure, i said goodbye
but you let us die
buried alive
controversy
a choice made shortsightedly
you didn't fight for me
took flight from me
now all that's left is dust
where particles of us could be

// solid matter

i cried a tear for every word left unsaid

stay
i'm listening
i can be anything you need me to be
i love you
please don't leave

i collected each tear in a bottle
and tossed it in the ocean
maybe the waves will carry the message
to the next girl who needs to hear it

// message in a bottle

a reminder that your heart was never meant for your sleeve
it's tucked nicely within your rib cage for good reason
so every bone can shield it from men who impersonate love
but penetrate you with toxins

// protect it at all costs

the chills
the obsession
the spiral
n o c o n t r o l
a loss
once loved
a love
now lost
i n s o m n i a
one-hundred
        ninety-nine
                ninety-eight
                        ninety-seven
                                ninety-six
is this sadness or exhaustion?
it's driving me mad
relentless thoughts
try counting backwards
from one hundred again

// counting sheep

why is it easier to write now
the ink is practically jumping out of my pen to kiss the paper
why can't i find the right words in joy
i guess that's the silver lining in all this
in the falling
       the euphoria
             the oblivion
                    the breaking
i'm writing again
maybe art will come of it

// i'll let you know if it's all worth it

it took me ten years to shed the layers of myself that were touched by you. ten years to shed the layers i outgrew.

you had this way of keeping me in a box. granted, i made a safe home there with you. we built a sacred space together, within those four walls. i was wary about it at first. but you kept reassuring me, we'd leave the box here and there. go on adventures. eventually those promises of adventure turned into echoes and faint hums. your box won, it confined me.

like i said, it took me ten years before i reached for a box cutter. and when i did, the universe applauded me. i took the first step to destroy the box and the universe moved me two more. i was never made for your box. there's an extraordinary world beyond it, one that has a divine plan for me.

// setting fire to cardboard boxes

her untamed flyaway hairs said
i am tired
            i am exhausted
                        i am overwhelmed
but I am surviving the chaos
and that is enough for now

// survival

healing

it's autumn. the seasons have cycled once more and you have found yourself alone, once again.

you say you've forgotten what it feels like to be loved.

you really think your mind forgets what love is when he leaves? because you have not been held? because no one has longed for you?

dear sister he is not love.

and i hope you see that with time. in time you will somehow find it in you to rise out of bed when your heart only wants to ache. you will laugh at yourself for the first time in months. you will laugh with your friends. maybe you'll even climb a mountain. at the top, you'll rest in your hammock and read poetry. you will accomplish what you never thought possible. art will come of it, the kind that surprises you, because you didn't know it was in you. you'll dream, so vividly - because he's free from your brain. you'll play the ukulele until your fingers hurt.

someday soon you'll wash your hair, until then fill your belly with the sweetest chocolate you can find. you will forget him soon, but i promise you have not forgotten what love is, just because he left.

// self love

write poetry until you love yourself again. write it backwards. then two times the speed. crinkle that shit up. this is therapy. toss it out. start over. in fact, start over as many times as you need.

remember you have no ties to chronological order. tell the story starting in the middle if it suits you. scribble, scribble, scribble.

forget order. art is born in chaos, so go on a frenzy. refuse to write in any color that's not bright teal or green envy. scrawl every letter with too much force if you have to. break through the paper. if that's what it takes to have an actual break through.

throw it away if you hate it. start over. pick your pen back up. pick your damn self back up.

// written therapy

sunday mornings were different then
waking from my dreams with a sort of amnesia
that is until the morning rain
and the rhythm of his chest
made music that reminded me
i was someone's sunday best

// looking back on it all

if he has your broken heart in his hands, let him fly
at least then your heart can see the world from the sky

// and he once said you deserve the world

if i am fragile
it is only like glass
which gets sharper
when it shatters

// deep cuts

for two days
i wrote
       and i wrote
           and i wrote
and there's nothing to show of it
for no paper could withstand
the force of my hand

// blue ink

i'm back in my writing spot
forcing my hand to write
picking through the ashes of my thoughts
and the remnants of my heart
why does it feel so unfamiliar here?
so hard to lift my pen...
these ashes, these remnants, this foreign land
all that remains here is my shadow
and an old relentless muse
this is no longer my space
i keep shedding

// cobra

i tried to sleep you away
but closed eyes are no defense against
a wandering mind

// three a.m.

the act of unloving, i think
was even more revealing
than the falling part
how i was able to stand up
place bandages on my swollen knees
and walk away unbroken

// numb limbs, full heart

loneliness is a notorious liar
whose dearest trick
is making you believe
you are not loved and never will be

// do not believe him

despite her flowing tears
and the burden of yesteryear
she will rise and roar
for all to hear

// lion

powers, like venom euphoric, momentum
then nothing but haze, a mere shadow of a face
wandering earth's darkest corners
solemn whispers from trees
a golden compass
emerges from the soil
what's lost can be found
so this route wasn't yours for the taking
don't fret my dear, two steps back
is a brand new awakening

// golden compass

most of those thoughts i've worked out by now
mind races until i let them drown out
a few deep breaths usually do the trick
a sweet self-reminder, *i am enough*
also helps with the ridding of it
the thoughts i can handle
the dreams though
the dreams are another beast
and they take no prisoners

// a quiet mind, a roaring heart

that she was so entirely whole
despite her scattered thoughts
is what made her so extraordinary

// one-of-a-kind mind

for as long as you are holding the hand of fear
you will never know the freedom of trust
you have to let go
       you have to let go
            you have to let go

// fear's hand

there is no dwelling
that can house both fear and faith

// one of them will prevail

i am not sorry for the person i have become. call me anything with roots but a wallflower, for i have spent years growing and learning about my heart's deepest desires, and they are no longer afraid of the limelight.

i spent countless hours saying yes, whatever you want, however you please. compromising my own being. but i am finally starting to see that my cup need not be emptied. i promise, i will do everything in my power to keep my heart fed.

// an ode to the things that fuel my soul, may we never lose sight of each other again.

you hear a lot about walls coming down in love. this is not prose for that kind of love.

because sometimes when your walls are down, you're abandoned. and you lose yourself. no, this is definitely not prose about that kind of love.

this is an ode to the builders. to the people that come into your life while you're vulnerable or broken and help you make something from nothing. to the ones who see your potential, value your worth, and help you build a stronger foundation from the rubble and the ashes.

to the friends and new lovers who show you more passion and respect than the wall bulldozer ever did. who, if even for a moment, build you a home in their arms, while you're repairing yours. to the fleeting moments. to the phoenix rising.

// phoenix

it's all coming back to me now.
the fire, the passion, the joy in the little things.
i've made space for it all to return.
because i've released the energy that no longer served me.
the washed up, drained energy i relied on to serve you.
i'm finding my home again.
and you're but a stranger in this house now.
the walls won't even whisper of you.

// the return

manifesting

can you feel it
are you awakening
free from the trappings you were bound to
can you feel the vibrations
the rhythms of each being in this new dimension

// the harmony of manifestation

universe, i am listening
i am ready to allow you to create through me
i will be the vessel
i will carry the message

// what do i need to hear

she retreated to the roof of her castle
not for a prince to rescue her
but to feel closer to the sky
to feel the vibrance of the sun
the vulnerability of the rain
and to see the earth like birds do

// once upon a time

i know better now
than to let my will interfere with destiny
i need to let what's meant to be, be
why push something beautiful away
just because it wasn't what you envisioned
you don't destroy abstract art
you cherish it

// destiny's painting

trust everything happens for a reason
even if you're not sure what it is
invest your heart in your life
never abandon it in hers or his
trust the path, breathe, just be
and if they ask, tell them
i'm loving me

// how to let go

there's a deep serenity in solitude
a peaceful, comforting silence
your thoughts no longer fighting to be heard
your heart no longer empty

// alone not lonely

follow your heart
especially when it leads you
straight to the forest
once there
dance along with your heart
listen to its sweet melody
hear how it syncs with the forest
seek out the other synchronized souls
breathe in and look around

// this is where you feel alive

and so it turns out
our intuition was god's portal
into our hearts and minds
and that's why we were told
to listen to it

// the secret

do not rush
do not impose
give your soul space
to play and grow
you are on universe time
trust the pendulum
and watch for synchronicity

// like clockwork

it's always dream big. but what about the finite details? sometimes the smallest things are weighing heaviest on our hearts. maybe we should start by dreaming small. taking note of the themes and stories we're telling ourselves. listen to what's going on in our own heads and hearts.

// dream small

to have patience and make room for growth
to be forgiving in the face of fear
to find comfort in the steady, in the slow
to breathe serenity in and uncertainty out
to show my spirit love
to leave footprints in the sand
so other souls can follow

// promises to self when the world is on fire

the sun is rising
i'm chasing hippocrene
trying to find a reason
trying to find a meaning
walking hand in hand
with a feeling

// hearts and hippocrene

honesty
keeps me
breathing
freely

// fresh air

trust your intuition
freedom is coming to fruition
identify connections
even in opposite directions
when one's trust must be earned
your instincts should you turn
soul, mind, body are attuned
go on, howl at the moon

// wolf

i don't have to sail across the sea
or journey to another moon
to find a miraculous love
honey all I need is a seed
and a little rain

// tiny miracles

just speak it into existence
put it in the universe
ask for what you need
pray for clarity

// mother gaia will lead you

my creativity
has led me
into a miraculous world
of self-forgiveness

// where my inner child can run free

you'd be surprised how the universe expands
folds and looks out for you, after you choose
when you take the first step, you are carried two more

// something or someone is looking out for you

i thought a lot about the last poem in this collection. how i should leave you, reader, with something to hold onto. as much as i wanted to tell you something profound or new, i think, instead the lesson is tried and true.

you will wander. you will fall. you will love and break and heal and love all over again. there will be hearts that come and go. souls who stay with you for a season. and some who stay longer than they should. there will be lovers who tear you down. and lovers who build you back up.

but the only heart that is constant, belongs to you. so keep it happy.

// love yourself first, sweet friend

so then tell me, if love is what you want from the universe,
will it begin in your hands?

gratitudes

thank you to my best friend, *dani day*, for being my encourager, editor, and personal hype woman. i couldn't have done this without you. thank you for believing in my wildest dreams.

thank you to my mom, *jodi short*, for being my cheerleader and inspiring me to finally get this collection out into the world.

thank you to *jamie boucher*, for capturing the essence of my poems and creating hearts of the earth's beautiful cover art.

thank you to *austie baird*, for taking a chance on this manuscript and giving me the opportunity to publish my words.

and thank you to you, *dear reader*, for your reading eyes and your open heart.

Morgan Short is a storyteller, marketer, oneironaut, and emerging poet from Inver Grove Heights, Minnesota. Prior to debuting Hearts of the Earth, Morgan's words were published in three A.B.Baird anthologies including Splintered Souls, under the alias M.R.S. With a degree in Journalism - Strategic Communications from the University of Wisconsin-Madison, Morgan has always been interested in finding and telling stories that move people.

For more incredible and inspiring words from Morgan, follow her on Instagram @morganraeshel_poems or on her website: www.morganraeshalshort.com

Made in the USA
Monee, IL
26 May 2021